STUFF DUTCH PEOPLE LIKE

presents

Praise for Stuff Dutch People Like

"A huge hit, hilarious."
AD

"For the Dutch, the book offers surprising - and
sometimes disturbing - insights."
NRC

"Extremely popular...especially among the Dutch."
NOS
(Het oog)

STUFF DUTCH PEOPLE SAY

A celebration of the weird, wacky and wonderful things Dutch people say

Colleen Geske

Stuff Dutch People Say

Copyright © 2015 by Colleen Geske

Words by Colleen Geske
Design by Putri Febriana
Edits by Tricia & Allan Geske
Production by Moses Faleafaga

Published in the Netherlands by Stuff Dutch People Like

Some of the material in this book may have originally appeared, in different form, on the popular blog StuffDutchPeopleLike.com

Photograph credits can be found on page 202

ISBN 9789082133622

Printed in the EU

10 9 8 7 6 5 4 3 2 1

www.stuffdutchpeoplelike.com
www.facebook.com/stuffdutchpeoplelike
www.twitter.com/stuffdutchlike

For media inquiries, corporate & volume sales or any other request, please contact us at hello@stuffdutchpeoplelike.com

Stuff Dutch People Say

To the 16.99 million Dutchies and the 28 million people of Dutch descent spread across the globe:

"You ain't much if you ain't Dutch!"

Table of Contents

"Never make fun of someone who speaks broken English. It means they know another language."

H. Jackson Brown, Jr.

INTRODUCTION

'Dutch', 'Nederlands', 'Hollands', 'Vlaams', 'Gibberish', 'Gobbledygook' - call it what you will, the Dutch language is a mouthful. Many a foreigner find the Dutch to be an intriguing, yet difficult, bunch of people to understand - and this isn't even on account of their language! Add a hearty heap of their throaty vernacular to the mix and you will be left well and truly perplexed.

Broadly speaking, outside the Netherlands the Dutch language is relatively unknown to the rest of the world. Of course, it is also spoken in Belgium, Suriname and the Dutch Antilles (Aruba, Curaçao and Sint Maarten), but many a tourist has been utterly shocked to learn that the Dutch do indeed have their own language. And no, it isn't German.

They say that Dutch is probably the easiest language to learn if you are a native English speaker. Apparently if you know German, the task is even easier! I disagree. Knowledge of German and English have helped me out here and there, but it's also been a hindrance as the three languages have proven to be just a bit too similar for my brain to successfully compartmentalize.

3

It seems that whenever I'm stuck for a Dutch word, some inappropriate German word will sneakily barge into the conversation. This can indeed be funny until you are attempting to speak Dutch on national radio and the host proclaims '*Zee Germans are coming!*'

It's been widely said that during the Second World War the name of the Dutch seaside town *Scheveningen* was used to weed out any German spies posing as Dutchies. I'm not sure if that was the right choice of words, as I mastered *Scheveningen* years ago. Try me on one of those massively long Dutch words or a sentence that has far too many guttural-sounding 'g's and things go utterly awry.

Take for instance, the longest word in the Dutch dictionary: '*Meervoudigepersoonlijkheidsstoornissen*'. Weighing in at 38 letters, the Dutch word for 'multiple personality disorders' is sure to raise eyebrows and tie tongues amongst the Dutch and non-Dutch alike! Why use three words when you can just go and stick 'em all together? Or how about the poetic phrase: *Wij smachten naar achtentachtig prachtige nachten bij achtentachtig prachtige grachten ("We long for eighty-eight wonderful nights at eighty-eight wonderful canals.")*. Now, that my friends, is a stymie, rhymey mouthful which certainly doesn't roll off the tongue easily.

4

Earlier this year, the 'Onze Taal' language institution conducted a study on the most difficult Dutch word to pronounce: '*meteorologisch*' (meteorological). Turns out, it's not quite as long as the examples above, but it does have me faltering: *Mete-oro-log-isch, mete-o-rol-o-gisch, Meteo-ro-lo-gisch*. Yep, I'm stumped.

Forget all this chit-chat about Dutch vocabulary and enunciation, that's only the beginning. Once you've mastered the basics, you'll find yourself moving onto a fanciful linguistic rollercoaster. We've put together only a sampling of the weird, wonderful and wacky things Dutch people say, and we're only getting started! Happy Reading!

The most famous handwritten text containing "Old Dutch" is:

"*Hebban olla vogala nestas hagunnan hinase hic anda thu, wat unbidan we nu?*", which translates to the poetic: "*All birds have started making nests, except me and you, what are we waiting for*".

This text dates from around the year 1100 AD and is said to have been written by a Flemish monk. It was long thought to be the oldest specimen of Dutch text on record, however, an older text (describing the law of the Salic Franks who occupied an area that stretched from North Brabant to Northern France) dates from the 6th century. Regardless, *Hebban olla vogala*, is most certainly still the most *romantic* Old Dutch text in history!

Gezellig

Lekker

Borrel

MASTERING DUTCH, 3 WORDS AT A TIME

Only have time to learn a handful of Dutch? Then you've come to the right place! Read on to learn the 3 most important words in the Dutch language.

Before reading any further you need to learn 3 essential Dutch words if you plan on spending any time visiting, touring or living in the Netherlands. These 3 critical words (*gezellig, lekker* and *borrel*) will serve you well. In fact, if you are lucky you may even stumble across a *lekker gezellige borrel* or two, during your stay!

Gezellig

Spend any time in the Netherlands and you will quickly learn that Dutch people love this perplexing guttural-sounding word. The Dutch are fiercely proud of this word and everything it represents. *Gezelligheid* is actually the modern day "religion" of the Dutch. They love it, they need it, and they respect it.

Don't be surprised if the Dutch ask you (over and over) if you know the word and then, if you know how to pronounce it! The pronunciation, it turns out, is actually the easiest part.

The tricky part is actually finding its English translation as *cosy, quaint, comfortable, familiar* and *friendly* all come up short. *Gezellig* is actually a feeling and we all know how hard feelings can be to describe - just ask my two-year-old!

Dutch people tend to evaluate just about everything on its particular level of *gezelligheid*. A place can be gezellig, a room can be *gezellig*, a person can be *gezellig*, an evening can be *gezellig*. Heck, Dutch women have even been known to describe giving birth as *gezellig*!

The good news is that even if you stay in the Netherlands for only a short amount of time, *gezellig* and its accompanying state-of-mind are sure to rub off on you. You still might not be able to translate the word perfectly into your own language, but chances are one day it will suddenly dawn on you that the place, the company, or the moment you are in is truly *gezellig*, and that will be worth more than a thousand words – in any language!

Lekker

This seemingly innocent word is ubiquitous in the Netherlands. *Lekker* in its original form refers to food and can be translated into tasty or yummy (the same as the German and Belgian word). Over time, however, the Dutch have taken some liberties with the word and now use it to describe, well, just about everything! A warm meal on a cold autumn day can of course be *lekker*, but so can a feeling, an experience, a place and even a person!

"Lekker ding": This expression is usually used when you think someone is hot (not necessarily said directly to them ☺).

11

VOEL JE LEKKER

met een mooi zomers kleurtje

Dove

DOVE
SUNSHINE
BODY
LOTION

tijd voor echte schoonheid op dove.com

Lekker is a highly versatile little word. Dutch people use it in endless instances, but beware, the original translation does not always hold true!

Expression	Literal translation	Actual meaning
Lekkere broodjes	Tasty sandwiches	Tasty sandwiches
Lekker rustig	Yummy calm	Pleasantly calm
Lekker weer	Tasty weather	Great weather
Niet lekker	Not yummy	Not nice, not well
Slaap lekker	Sleep tasty	Sleep well
Lekker ruim	Tasty space	Lots of space/room

Borrel

Dutch people love a good *borrel*. Or should I rephrase, they love a good excuse to have a *borrel*. How can one appropriately translate the Dutch word *borrel*?

It's much more than just "drinks", yet not quite as formal an affair as a "function" or "reception".

> According to our good ol' friend Mr. Wikipedia, a *borrel* is:
>
> *1. an informal designation for a small glass of spirits*
> *2. an informal social gathering of a select (invited) group,*
> *often with a theme*

The second definition is fairly accurate but still not exactly right, which is why you will often hear many an English-speaker using the Dutch word *borrel* instead of any old english term (e.g "Are you going to that *borrel* tonight?").

Along with the word *borrel*, comes a slew of other *borrel*-y words: you can attend a *kerstborrel* and eat *borrelnootjes* and *borrelhapjes* while sitting at a *borreltafel* while engaging in a little *borrelpraat* and sipping from your *borrelglas*. Got it? Good!

LOST IN TRANSLATION

Sometimes literal translations from Dutch to English make sense. Sometimes they result in sheer hilarity. Read on for our pick of the funniest translated Dutch words.

HANDSCHOENEN
(HAND) (SHOES)
=
Gloves

As you may have already heard, the Dutch certainly do not beat around the bush. This does have a plus side as it conveniently applies, not only to their direct behaviour, but also their use of language.

Why complicate things when you can just literally spell them out? For instance, who needs a fancy (rather nonsensical) word like "glove" when you are simply looking for something to keep your hands warm (sort of like what shoes do for your feet!). No need to go about confusing us foreigners with more words to learn. Similarly, when boating through the canals of Amsterdam I discovered that only one word is needed to discuss the depth of the murky bicycle-laden waters: *diep* (deep). Slap a little prefix in front of it, and you've got its handy companion *ondiep* (undeep). Again, no need to go and learn something new. ☺

SCHOONMOEDER
(CLEAN) (MOTHER)
=
Mother-in-law

Schoonmoeder

Schoonmoeder is the Dutch word for mother-in-law. Oddly enough the literal English translation for this term is "clean-mother"! Does this Dutch word, in fact, refer to the frantic cleaning required prior to an impending visit from your mother-in-law, or her holier-than-thou attitude toward obsessive cleanliness?!

Many a (Dutch) mother-in-law has been known to either:

1. bluntly remark on said daughter/son-in-law's lack of hygienic standards, or
2. take it upon themselves to clean and/or rearrange kitchen cupboards to a more "useful" state

Truth be told, the actual origin likely has little to do with the subject of cleanliness and more to do with the lesser known meaning of the word *schoon*: "beautiful/fair". Similar to the French term *belle-mere*, schoonmoeder thus refers to your "beloved" mother-in-law whether, or not, she truly is "beloved" is a whole other story!

21

TOILETBRIL
(TOILET) (GLASSES)
=
Toilet Seat

Toiletbril

Let it be said that the Dutch have interesting toilet habits. To start with, their WC (Wash Closet, that is) is normally separated from the rest of its bathroom companions accompanied only by the teeny tiniest of sinks. Peer into any North American bathroom and by contrast you will find the shiny porcelain sink, vanity, shower, bath and toilet all living happily together.

Now to make matters even more confusing, the Dutch have gone and given their toilet seat the most oddest of names: *toiletbril*! Yes, you read that correctly, the Dutch word for 'toilet seat' is in fact... toilet glasses!

What the heck do *glasses* have to do with a toilet?
Some would say that the "*bril*" part comes from the shape of said toilet seat: resembling a spectacle of sorts hovering over the "eye" of the toilet bowl. Now this would be a very simple and convenient explanation. However, I would argue that the truth is likely a step further. We at SDPS believe the word '*toiletbril*' has more to do with the Dutch toilet itself! Read on...

Nowadays many modern Dutch homes and apartments have toilets similar to those found the world over, but a *true* Dutch toilet, an *original* Dutch toilet, is a peculiar sight! These toilets are instead equipped with a ledge or shelf of sorts rather than a water-filled bowl, lending itself to a whole new world of exploration. You can still find these beauties all over the country (*if you don't believe me I'll take you to my first apartment in Amsterdam's Oud-Zuid*).

If you've ever done your business in one, you'll know immediately what I am talking about. The toilet's shelf serves as a platter to display the contents of your bowels for closer examination. *Corn for lunch? Why, yes, how did you know?*

Grossed out yet!? Well, I certainly was, and I will never forget hearing my Canadian sister-in-law's loud gasp when first using my toilet! However, when I learnt the word "*toiletbril*" it all started to make sense: put on your toilet glasses and start the inspection!!

PINDAKAAS
(PEANUT) (CHEESE)
=
Peanut butter

Pindakaas

We all know the Dutch are obsessed with dairy (*in fact per capita milk consumption in the Netherlands is one of the highest in the world, surpassed only by Finland and Sweden*), but what does peanut butter have to do with cheese?!

Depending on who you ask, you'll get a few explanations as to how this name came about. As with most things, the truth probably lies somewhere in the middle. Let's look at some nutty facts:

The oldest use of the Dutch word 'pindakaas' dates from 1855. The word 'piendakaas' appeared in the Surinamese dictionary at this time and referred to a large block of crushed peanuts that locals sliced in a similar way to that of a block of cheese and ate on bread.

Canadian Marcellus Edson of Montreal, Quebec, was the first to officially patent peanut butter in 1884. *Blame Canada*.

 January 24 is National Peanut Butter day in the United States. *Why? I have absolutely no idea.*

 Peanut butter, as we now know it, was introduced to the Dutch market by the brand Calvé in 1948.

 It was, however, not possible to market it under the name of 'pindaboter' due to the 'Butterlaw' (I kid you not!). This 'Butterlaw' (originating from 1889) stipulated, in short, that only butter could call itself butter.

 Dutch peanut butter was thus marketed as 'pindakaas'. Perhaps referencing the old 'peanut cheese' snack from Suriname. We'll never know.

It turns out that the 'Butterlaw' is surprisingly no longer in effect! Peanut butter is now finally free to rightfully call itself 'pindaboter'... however the change has yet to come. I suppose after 67 years there are more pressing issues in the world!

Helaas Pindakaas

SPIJKERBROEK
(NAIL) (PANTS)
=
Jeans

Spijkerbroek

The majority of Dutchies have likely worn *"spijkerstoffen"* their entire lives. They've probably got up in the morning, slipped on a pair of *spijkerbroek*, ate their morning *broodje*, and cycled to work - all without questioning the odd name of their universally popular pants.

For some reason, I just don't have that luxury. The first time I heard the word I paused, scratched my head and thought a little bit before yelling into my closet "*Where oh where does this strange word come from?!?*'

You see, the English translation is 'nail pants' (as in hammer-and-nail!) and my favourite pair of G-star jeans are certainly less painful than the name implies.

So what is the origin of this word? And what do nails have to do with jeans? To fully decipher this linguistic riddle we will need to travel back in time: to the mid-1800 gold rush days where a Bavarian immigrant and merchant, Levi Strauss, decided to respond to the demand for sturdier miners clothing in San Francisco by developing a pair of denim overalls.

Although the jeans were pretty sturdy they still could not fully withstand the heavy demands of the miners, so Levi partnered with a Latvian-born tailor, Jacob Davis, who suggested the final critical ingredient: nails! By bolting the material together at the seams with rivets (*klinknagels*) the two shrewd entrepreneurs designed the perfect pants and quickly patented their invention in 1873.

So you see, the Dutch word is in fact less silly than it seems, as *spijkers* refers to those now fashionable bolts holding your beloved pants together. Chances are you might just be staring down at those handy little "nails" right now. See 'em?

BOTERHAM
(BUTTER) (HAM)
=
Sandwich

A TALE OF TWO SANDWICHES

The Dutch workplace cafeteria offers endless learning opportunities. Observe cultural quirks from a distance while munching quietly on your own, or throw yourself in at the deep end and join your colleagues for a totally immersive experience!

I chose the latter, and on one of my first lunch meetings with a Dutch colleague (*let's call him Jaap*) things quickly went awry.

Jaap : *"Are you having a boterham for lunch?"*

Me : *"Nah, I'm not such a fan of ham."*

Jaap looking perplexed : *"Ok, what are you going to have then?"*

Me : *"Hmmm, maybe just a sandwich."*

35

Jaap looking even more perplexed : *"So you are having a boterham."*

Me : *"Nope."*

Jaap (now kinda annoyed) pointing at my tuna sandwich : *"Well there's a boterham on your plate"*

Me : Silence. [Maybe if I don't answer this conversation will be over…].

As you may have surmised, the Dutch curiously use the word "butter ham" for sandwich. I believe this is the case simply to confuse all non-Dutchies and make lunch time a little more fun.

Was Jaap aware of my rookie misunderstanding and engaged in the conversation for his own personal amusement? I'll never know.

Now, I hear you all, shaking your heads and shouting "*Boterham* makes MUCH more sense than "sandwich"!! Well, just this once, I may have to agree with you. But whilst agreeing with you, I will tell you a little story:

Once upon a time there was a man named John Montagu (1718-1792). This John Montagu happened to be a ferocious gambler. During marathon gambling sessions he was said to eat slices of cold meat between bread in order to avoid taking breaks to eat a proper meal. Mr Montagu happened to also be the Fourth Earl of Sandwich, thus the name of his odd snack, the sandwich, took hold.

So yes, dear readers, *boterham* does indeed make more sense than the word sandwich. Dutch 1: 0 English.

MIERENNEUKER
(ANT) (F@#KER)
=
Somebody who cares too much about details

Mierenneuker

So I'm sitting in a meeting, a somewhat civilized affair, and my colleagues are disagreeing (once again) about a rather trivial detail. The disagreement is jovial but passive aggressive jibes are flying from both sides. I decide not to get involved and instead stare out the window in the hope that it will soon pass. The beautiful thing about meetings in a foreign language is that you can tune out the chatter much easier (than in your own native tongue). Soon enough I've drifted away and all that's left is a soothing hum of throaty Dutch consonants... until... I am suddenly brought back into reality with the recognition of the Dutch word *neuker* (excuse my language, translation: f@#ker)!

You see, colleague #1 has just called colleague #2 a *mierenneuker*. I immediately understand both parts of this word a) mieren = ant and b) neuker = f@#ker, but have curiously never heard the pairing before!

I scan the faces of both colleagues to gauge whether this statement was a lighthearted joke or a nasty insult. The non-verbal cues suggest it lies somewhere in between. The meeting draws to an end and I race to my laptop to google "antf@#ker" as fast as my fingers can type. I just couldn't think of an appropriate way to interrupt the meeting to ask "*Excuse me. In what context does the 'f@#king of ants' have to do with our website?*" Some things, it seems, are better left unsaid.

> Google, however, never fails to be my trusty cultural translator and quickly reveals that:
>
> a) "antf@#ker" is indeed a common Dutch expression, and
> b) being an "antf@#ker" is to be overly obsessed with small details; an equivalent to the English "nitpicker" or "hairsplitter".

I lean back from my computer, satisfied that the two hours spent in yet another Dutch meeting were not in vain: I've learnt a handy new Dutch word, and the fact that the proclamation of a swear word - in any language - can still wake me out of the deepest of daydreams. Go figure.

In 2005 a motorist called a parking attendant a *mierenneuker* and received a €220 fine. The man refused to pay the fine and the case went to court. In his ruling the judge concluded that, after looking it up in a dictionary, *mierenneuker* wasn't necessarily an offensive term and that it could actually be considered a compliment. The case was thrown out. In the aftermath of the acquittal, *miereneuker* very quickly became the #1 epithet shouted at parking attendants on a regular basis.

EZELSBRUGGETJE
(DONKEY'S) (BRIDGE)
=
Mnemonic

Donkey's bridge

I was in the most unlikely of places, the south of France, when I first stumbled across a Dutch donkey's bridge. To clarify, I was studying for my final Italian exam. What possessed me to attempt to learn a third language (Italian) in my second language (French), I will never know. Needless to say, it wasn't coming easily but luckily my handsome Dutch study companion, Joris, made the task somewhat easier.

It was Joris, in fact, who suggested the solution could be found in a "donkey's bridge". "A whaat??" I proclaimed. Joris was quick to explain.

I learned the Dutch equivalent of a 'mnemonic' was the curiously named *ezelsbruggetje* (donkey's bridge). However, no amount of *mnemonic* helped me to learn Italian!

Now for those of you who have neither heard of a donkey's bridge or a mnemonic (pronounced "ne-mon-ic"), let me explain:

Mnemonics assist the memory by using a system of rhymes, rules, phrases, diagrams, acronyms and other devices – to help you learn, remember and memorize information. A mental tool, of sorts, to assist you in making a connection between one idea and another.

You probably know a few mnemonics without even knowing it! Take for instance, the colours of the rainbow. Most English-speakers know of the man named: Roy G Biv. The letters of his name, spelling out the order and colours of the rainbow: **R**ed, **O**range, **Y**ellow, **G**reen, **B**lue, **I**ndigo, **V**iolet.

I can't say that the above has served me all that well over the years, but I suppose it could help on a potential Jeopardy appearance.

Now to get back to the story of those Dutchies and their crazy use of the word *ezelsbruggetje*. The story goes that donkeys are particularly fearful of water. To get a donkey to cross the countryside it was often necessary to build temporary plank bridges over gaps and ditches, creating handy shortcuts. This is how *ezelsbruggetje* came to mean memory tricks using shortcuts.

Once a donkey finds his way over water the first time (be it by bridge or stone or path) it never forgets its route again.

I have yet to ride a donkey through a water laden terrain, so I cannot fully vouch for either explanation but it is definitely on my "to-do" list. I'll report back shortly on my findings!

OUR **TOP 5** DUTCH 'DONKEY BRIDGES'

1

Prinsen Kopen Heren Schoenen

This one has certainly helped me out while navigating Amsterdam's canals by bike! The order of canals from the outermost: **P**rinsengracht, **K**eizersgracht, **H**erengracht and **S**ingel.

2

TV Tas

This one is used to remember the names of the Dutch Wadden islands: **T**exel, **V**lieland, **T**erschelling, **A**meland and **S**chiermonnikoog.

3

Niet Op Zondag Werken

Used to remember the cardinal directions in Dutch: **N**oord, **O**ost, **Z**uid, **W**est.

4 Ding flof bips
The first letters of the 12 countries that initially joined the Euro on January 1st 2002. (**D**uitsland, **I**erland, **N**ederland, **G**riekenland, **F**inland, **L**uxemburg, **O**ostenrijk, **F**rankrijk, **B**elgië, **I**talië, **P**ortugal, **S**panje)

5 Mijn Goudvis Bas Eet Haast Nooit Chocolade Pudding
The countries of mainland Central America, from top left to right bottom: **M**exico, **G**uatemala, **B**elize, **E**l Salvador, **H**onduras, **N**icaragua, **C**osta Rica, **P**anama.

SCHILDPAD
(SHIELD) (TOAD)
=
Turtle

LET'S VISIT A DUTCH ZOO

When learning a new language you are often confronted with some rather infantile reading material and for some reason this material always seems to involve an awful lot of animals. Thus my beginner's Dutch was highly appropriate for a visit to the zoo but utterly useless, well pretty much, anywhere else. Going on a Sub-Saharan safari? Take me along! I'm your perfect companion!! I'll name all the animals for you in several European languages. Heck, I'll even count 'em!

While learning a plethora of new animal names, I also encountered some wonderfully whimsical Dutch words. Take, for example, the humble turtle. In English, the word comes from the French *tortue, tortre* but the Dutch have a beautifully descriptive term: *schildpad*. The literal translation in this case is "shield toad".

I'm not sure about you, but when I first heard this word I was immediately taken to a storybook forest scene with a little naked toad holding an oversized shield. Realizing he could protect himself indefinitely with this handy shield, he decided to throw it on his back and thus transform himself from a lowly toad to a majestic turtle! Ok, ok, I digress, but you get the idea: the Dutch word is much more imaginative!

The "shield toad" isn't the only animal to be having so much fun. Check out a few of our favourites:

LUIPAARD
(LAZY) (HORSE)
=
Leopard

ZEEWOLF
(SEA) (WOLF)
=
Catfish

GORDELDIER
(BELT) (ANIMAL)
=
Armadillo

TUINSLANG
(GARDEN) (SNAKE)
=
Hose

BRANDSLANG
(FIRE) (SNAKE)
=
Fire Hose

PAARDENBLOEM
(HORSE) (FLOWER)
=
Dandelion

SPEAKING IN EXPRESSIONS

It's been said that, on average, 30% of a language is idiom and expressions. Dutch is actually 98.7%. Well maybe not that high, but be prepared for utter confusion when cows, monkeys, windmills and weather barge into your everyday casual conversations.

"I'd lived in Amsterdam 10 years and considered myself fluent in Dutch, as did many of my friends. Then I went to a publishing bash at the West Indischhuis in Amsterdam where I touched in speech (raakte in gesprek) with a philologist from the UVA. After we'd exchanged mythologies for a while he stopped me; "It's weird", he said, "you speak fluent Dutch, and yet you don't speak Dutch at all!"

Confused, I asked him to explain. "Your Dutch is superb, but you use absolutely no idiom, and Dutch is at least 50% idiom." He proceeded to explain and from that evening I changed my approach to the language. That was 27 years ago."

From a SDPL fan

Alsof er een engeltje over je tong piest
(As if an angel is peeing on your tongue)
=
Someone who really enjoys his meal!

Een slag van den molen weg hebben
(To have been hit by a windmill)
=
To act crazy/unintelligent

SPEAKING IN EXPRESSIONS

I had a colleague who almost exclusively spoke in Dutch expressions. Some would see this as charming, perhaps poetic, however the problem was that these expressions were Dutch ones literally translated into English. The result was a mix of utterly odd and non-sensical English phrases! I heard of cows being pulled out of ditches, heads being chopped off in cornfields, the making of chocolate and monkeys, of course. Yes, lots of monkeys.

There is no doubt that the Dutch love their expressions. The Dutch language is littered with hundreds and hundreds of expressions and idioms. Try having a chat with any Dutch person and you will see that expressions make their way into, literally, every conversation. For us non-Dutchies, this can be a challenge. You think you've mastered the language, and then suddenly you hear about someone being 'hit on the head with a windmill', or 'having butter on their head' or worse, 'falling into the house with a door'. In that moment, with the conversation rapidly progressing you need to decipher whether a) these odd occurrences really did happen or b) they're just another Dutch wacky figure of speech!

It's been said that on average 30% of any language is made up of idioms and expressions. I would venture to say that the Dutch clock in a lot higher. It may make for some initial confusion but overall it lends to a beautifully rich and imaginative experience! Dive in and enjoy the ride!

Met de deur in huis vallen
(To fall with the door into the house)
=
To get straight to the point

Now the monkey comes out of the sleeve

MONKEY BUSINESS

Last time I checked, monkeys were not indigenous to the Netherlands, yet by a sampling of the country's expressions you would certainly think so! Why is this flat little water-logged country so obsessed with monkey references? Your guess is as good as mine!

Nu komt de aap uit de mouw

Translation

Now the monkey comes out of the sleeve

Meaning

Similar to the English expression "to let the cat out of the bag"; the moment that a hidden motive or the truth behind something is revealed

History

In the past, street artists would often perform tricks by hiding a monkey in their coats. At the end of the performance the monkey would "come out of the sleeve" and reveal the trick!

Al draagt een aap een gouden ring, het is en blijft een lelijk ding

Translation

Even a monkey with a golden ring is still ugly

Meaning

Similar to the English expression "a pig in lipstick"; used to convey the message that superficial or cosmetic changes are futile at disguising the true nature of a person or thing.

Een broodjeaapverhaal

Translation

A monkey-sandwich story

Meaning

An untrue story, an "urban legend"

History

The term comes from the title of a 1978 book by Ethel Portnoy which was a collection of urban legends (and contained one about an Amsterdam restaurant that served monkey meat). Eww.

**A monkey with a golden ring
is still an ugly thing**

APENSTAARTJE
(LITTLE MONKEY) (TAIL)
=

Apenstaartje

Translation
Little monkey's tail
Meaning
The @ symbol!

Iemand met apenmunt betalen

Translation
To pay someone with monkey coins
Meaning
To fool someone with nice/flattering words

In de aap gelogeerd zijn

Translation
To lodge at the 'Monkey's'
Meaning
To be in trouble, to not be in a good place. Similar to the English expression "to be in in dire straits"
History
The origin of this expression is not certain, but many believe it may refer to an old inn/tavern called "The Monkey" which was found in the center of Amsterdam in the 17th century.

Various explanations exist as to why "The Monkey" inn would have been associated with trouble or negative consequences:

The inn was particularly unpleasant and sailors who stayed there were probably desperate, as a stay could result in fleas, lice and so on.

Sailors staying/drinking at the inn could often not pay their bills and some were said to have literally paid with a monkey (from their exotic travels). The inn was rumoured to have monkeys on hand, and as monkeys often carry illnesses, staying there was a risk!

The VOC often recruited sailors at the inn by liberally offering free booze. Drunk men were said to have signed binding contracts only to wake up in the morning and realized what they had done!

Regardless of which story is closest to the truth, "staying at the Monkey" was certainly not without consequence! Buyer beware!

Als apen hoger klimmen willen, ziet men gauw hun blote billen

Translation

If monkeys want to climb higher, we will soon see their bare bums

Meaning

Similar to the English expression to "bite off more than you can chew"; if you try to do more than you can, you will end up making a fool of yourself.

It's raining pipe-stems

WEATHER OR NOT...

I thought Canadians were the most weather-obsessed people... that was, until I moved to the Netherlands. Turns out there is another nation that spends even more time endlessly discussing the past, present and future weather conditions. Having lived nearly 10 years in this meteorologically fickle country, I now understand why. Unlike Canada's rather persistent weather states (cold, cold and colder), weather in the Netherlands can turn on a dime. You can have brilliant sunshine one moment, followed by intense winds and hail, which can then miraculously return to blue skies all in the matter of a short morning. For a nation whose history (and economy) was based on seafaring and agriculture you can understand why this mattered, and more importantly, why it was so often the topic of conversation.

75

Yes, my Dutch friends, the truth is out: other nations do not nearly discuss the weather as much as you do. The Spanish along the Costa Brava don't have daily chitchat on how lovely the sunshine feels on their sun-kissed faces or tapas-filled bellies. With that being said, they also don't have nearly as many weather-related expressions! Let's look at a few of our favourites:

Het regent pijpenstelen

Translation

It's raining pipe-stems

I've been known to casually throw this expression into a conversation with a complete stranger at a tram stop just because I really like the visual imagery it evokes. Can you see it now? A sky filled with the long stems of colourful little pipes, perfectly illustrating the intense Dutch rain falling down in sheets.

Since the Netherlands does happen to have a LOT of rain, it's no surprise that there are equally a LOT of expressions about rain! To go a step further, there are also a LOT of expressions that start with "*It's raining [insert object]*".

LET'S LOOK AT A FEW MORE EXAMPLES :

 het regent koeiestaarten (It's raining cow tails!)

 het regent bakstenen (It's raining bricks!)

 het regent mollejongen/mollenjongen (It's raining boy moles!)

 het regent scheermessen (It's raining razors!)

 het regent telegraafdraden (It's raining telegraph wires!)

 het regent kopjes en schoteltjes (It's raining cups and saucers!)

77

Hondenweer

Translation

Dog's weather

What does a 'man's-best-friend' have to do with the weather? Or more particularly, with Dutch weather?! As with so many expressions the origin seems to be a bit muddled. At first glance the expression appears rather similar to the popular English idiom "It's raining cats and dogs", however, the Dutch expression seems to have its roots in two theories:

1. *hondenweer* might refer to the fact that in terrible weather only people with dogs (who need to do their business) venture out into the streets
2. *hondenweer* may actually be referring to the old Netherlands word *ondeweer* - which itself was used to describe bad weather

Regardless of the explanation, innocent Dutch doggies seem to have been inadvertently blamed for the nation's wet woes. I suppose we all need a scapegoat - or more appropriately - a "scape-dog"!

Niet van suiker zijn

Translation

Not made of sugar

I had only been living in Amsterdam for a few months when I first heard this expression. It was a rainy October day and I was due at a meeting shortly on the other side of town. The rain was pouring down and my colleague asked when I planned on leaving. Naively I suggested postponing the meeting due to the rain: *"We're not expected to travel in this weather, right?".* My colleague looked at me with an incredulous grin, *"Hah!! You're not made of sugar, are you?!".* I quickly gathered from her facial expression that this meant the meeting was most definitely still on!

Looking back, years later, I can see I got away lightly, as a little (or even a lot) of rain is, in no uncertain terms, NOT a suitable excuse for cancelling a meeting in the Netherlands.

I suppose when my colleague and I jumped on our bikes and cycled through the torrential Dutch rain, we could have been said to "have hair on our teeth"!

According to the *Fietsersbond* (the Dutch cyclists' union. Yes they have one!) 82% of Dutchies will persevere and cycle in "strong rain". The Dutch are a tough breed and when compared to their German neighbors, they appear even tougher: in the same study 40% of Germans said they would leave their bikes at home at the mere "sight of a rain cloud". *Oranje boven*!

Haar op de tanden hebben
(To have hair on one's teeth)
=
To be very sturdy/strong

To make an elephant out of a fly

JUST BE NORMAL ALREADY

Van een vlieg een olifant maken
Translation
To make an elephant out of a fly

Meaning
Don't make something out of nothing, similar to the English expression 'to make a mountain out of a molehill'.

Doe maar gewoon, dan doe je al gek genoeg
Translation
Act normal, that's crazy enough

Doe normaal
Translation
Be normal/stop acting crazy

There is no denying that Dutch people like to keep things "normal". The ubiquitous Dutch phrases *"Doe normaal"* and *"Doe maar gewoon, dan doe je al gek genoeg"* have been said to be the backbone of Dutch culture.

In a recent study, 9/10 Dutchies choose the latter expression to define their national character. But what do these expressions really mean, and where do they come from?

The idea of "being normal" and blending in with the crowd originates from the Dutch Calvinistic roots. Although no longer seen as an overtly religious nation, their Calvinist principles (hard-working, no-nonsense, equalitarian and modest) still shine through! It therefore comes as no surprise that so many Dutch expressions emphasize these traits, particularily those of being modest and equal to others. Be warned: you won't make any friends in the Netherlands by 'tooting your own horn'!

Hoge bomen vangen veel wind

Translation

High trees catch a lot of wind

Meaning

It's not necessarily a good thing to stand out in a crowd. People in a higher position of importance will garner more disdain and/or criticism

Steek je hoofd niet boven het maaiveld uit

Translation

Don't put your head above the cornfield

Variation :

Wie het hoofd boven het maaiveld uitsteekt, wordt zijn kop eraf gehakt

Translation

He who puts his head above the cornfield will have it chopped off

Meaning

It is better to blend in with the crowd. Don't draw unnecessary attention to yourself or your actions

Het zijn niet de slechtste vruchten waaraan de wespen knagen

Translation

It isn't the worst fruit that is eaten by wasps

Meaning

Good people are often subjected to the jealousy or envy of others. Unkind things are often said about good people

Eigen lof stinkt

Translation

Self-praise stinks

Meaning

Speaking highly of one's self gives a bad impression

As you can see, these phrases offer a cautionary tale against "standing out in a crowd" or "doing things differently". Contrary to the American ideal of differentiating yourself at all costs, the Dutch prefer to work hard, blend in, and be "normal". Self-congratulatory behaviour will make you no friends in the Lowlands.

**Als twee honden vechten om een been
loopt de derde ermee heen**
(When 2 dogs fight over a bone, a third dog
walks away with it alone)
=
Don't get into an argument,
because somebody else will benefit

He who has butter on his head
should stay out of the sun

MELK MOET!

You can tell a lot about a country by their expressions. Listen closely to the Dutch vernacular and you'll be sure to hear the constant moo-ing (or shall I say "boo-ing") of a Dutch dairy cow. Turns out there are as many expressions relating to cow's milk or dairy as there are calves grazing amongst the polders!

Wie boter op zijn hoofd heeft, moet uit de zon blijven

Translation

He who has butter on his head, should stay out of the sun

Meaning

Similar to the English expression "People in glass houses shouldn't throw stones". You should not criticize others unless you yourself are without fault.

History

The phrase is said to have been around since the 17th century, as it was found in a text by the famous Dutch poet Jacob Cats (1577-1660).

89

Why butter is referenced is largely unknown, although it may refer to when people would carry their groceries in baskets on their heads. Regardless, having butter melt on your face would make you look like a fool.

Je weet nooit hoe een koe en haas vangt

Translation

You never know how a cow catches a hare

Meaning

You never know how things will turn out; you can't predict the future; strange things can happen

Geduld, en gras zal melk worden

Translation

Patience and grass makes milk

Meaning

Patience leads to a good result; good things come to those who wait

You never know how a cow catches a hare

Met zijn neus in de boter vallen

Translation

To fall with your nose in butter

Meaning

To (luckily) be at the right place at the right time

Waarom ergens anders melk halen als je thuis een koe hebt

Translation

Why get milk from someone else when you have a cow at home

Meaning

Don't cheat on your partner; Don't go elsewhere for something you already have

Melk de koe, maar trek ze niet de spenen af

Translation

Milk the cow, but don't pull off her teats

Meaning

If you get greedy or overzealous you'll end up destroying the whole thing

Over koetjes en kalfjes praten

Translation

To talk about (small) cows and calves

Meaning

To talk about trivial matters

Oude koeien uit de sloot halen

Translation

To drag old cows out of the ditches

Meaning

To bring up old grudges/to resurrect past grievances

MORE WACKY EXPRESSIONS

Een kat in de zak kopen

Translation

To buy a cat in the bag

Meaning

To have been duped into buying something without inspecting it properly

Weten waar Abraham de mosterd haalt

Translation

To know where Abraham got the mustard from

Meaning

To have great insight into something

History

This expression likely has its source in the Old testament (Genesis 22:6), where Abraham is ordered to sacrifice his first born. He collects *mutsaard*, an old term for fire wood. Mutsaard over time likely bastardized to *mosterd*, et voila: another crazy Dutch expression!

To buy a cat in the bag

Ben je van de trap gevallen?

Translation

Did you fall down the stairs?

Meaning

A dutchie might ask you this odd question if you have had a rather drastic hair cut

History

The original version of the expression *Hij is van de trap gevallen en heeft zijn haar gebroken* (He fell down the stairs and broke his hair) was already in use in the 18th century.

Did you fall down the stairs?

1 april, kikker in je bil!

Translation

1st of April, frog in your butt!

Meaning

April fools!

History

In 1572, the Low countries were at the beginning of the Eighty Years' War of Independence against the occupying Spanish forces of Philip II. The 1st of April, 1572, marked a turning point in the uprising of what was to become the Netherlands. The city of Den Briel was recaptured by rebel forces.

The capture of Den Briel was thus a very important symbolic event and has been celebrated ever since. Dutch people took up a short rhyme to remember this event: "*Op 1 april verloor Alva zijn bril*", meaning "On April 1st, Alva lost his glasses," which is a pun on the word *bril*, Dutch for 'glasses', and the name of the town *Den Briel*. "Alva" referrs to Fernando Álvarez de Toledo, then the appointed Govenor of The Netherlands, who was replaced shortly afterwards. As one thing led to another, *bril* evolved to *bil* (butt)... and the silly joke "kikker in je bil" caught on!

1st of April, frog in your butt

Comments from our community

An American friend of mine complained to a Roermond hotelkeeper that the bathroom in his room was too small: "Not big enough to swing a cat in." The hotelkeeper looked soberly at him: "You're not allowed to have pets in this hotel."

It's probably an economical way of speaking. Why invent your own sentences if there already is an expression?

There are tons of expressions that don't make sense. Recently I met with a Dutch client (well known large bank) where a senior executive said, that we will have to do it with not one but two fingers in the nose. My English colleagues were totally shocked and were looking at me as they had no clue what he was referring to. Doing something "met je vinger in neus" is also something not to be translated, as it only expresses something that you can do it very easy without effort. Putting then two fingers in the nose is even less effort. After the explanation they just shook their heads in disbelief.

My manager once said to some Italian visitors: "I don't see any bears on the road". We've been using this phrase ever since!

One of the first phrases my husband taught me was "You can't pluck a bald chicken"

My favourite saying is: "Ze kunnen beter over je fiets lullen dan over je lul fietsen". Means, that it does not hurt you when they talk about you, (over je fiets lullen, talk about your bike), but the other way around does hurt (over je lul fietsen, bike over your penis)

My Father used the Dutch expression " the food is so good it's like an angel peeing on my tongue" on first meeting his future in-laws at Sunday dinner in Montreal. Grandpa laughed Grandma wasn't impressed! LOL

Hello
my name is
JAN

It has been said, "It ain't what they call you, it's what you answer to." Take a peek at the odd meanings of some popular Dutch names.

Would you describe yourself as a 'Nervous Nelly' (*an anxious person*), a 'Smart Alec' (*a know-it-all*) or a Jack-of-all-trades (*someone who can do a bit of everything*)?

Are you "In like Flynn"(*popular with the ladies*) or "Happy as Larry"(*content*)? In any case, we certainly hope you're not a 'Peeping Tom' (*pervert*) or end up a "Jane Doe"(*unidentified victim*)!

The English have a slew of phrases containing names, and it turns out the Dutch have their own variations as well! Here's our shortlist:

Vrolijke Frans	"Jolly Frans"	a cheerful person
Houten Klaas	"Wooden Klaas"	an awkward person
Jan Jansen	"John Doe"	the most common first and last name
Jan en Alleman	"John and Everyone"	meaning everybody/everyone
Jarige Jet		the birthday girl
Jarige Job		the birthday boy
Smeerkees	"Dirty Kees"	someone who gets dirty, needlessly, while doing a task
Mafkees	"Crazy Kees"	a goofball; a weirdo
Razende Roeltje	"Roaring Roland'	a very energetic person
Saaie Piet	"Boring Peter"	someone who is a bore
Ware Jacob	"True/real Jacob"	Mr. Right
Zeurpiet	"Sour Peter"	someone who complains a lot

Swearing with diseases

We f@#%ing hate it when people swear, except for the Dutch. They have a way with words like no other. We sh*# you not!

Swearing is universal; people have, and always will need a way to express themselves in the harshest linguistic way possible. Strong language often involves the naming and shaming of forbidden or highly-regarded societal pillars. Take for example, religion, both the swearing vernacular of the English and French (in particular French-Canadians) involve religious figures ('Jesus Christ!', 'For God's sake!') or items ('tabernacle!' - where you store the communion wafer, 'calice!' - the chalice of wine for communion).

Each nation has its own particular flare when it comes to swear words, however, common themes such as religion, sexuality, faeces… and well, mothers, run freely. Sexuality is obvious (*"go f@#K yourself"*, *"f@#K off"*, etc.) as are the references to morality. The latter seen in the numerous multi-lingual references to 'whores' (French: *putain*, Spanish: *puta* and *hijo de puta*, Italian: *puttana,* etc.)

Mothers seem to have been dragged into the fun, with references to *'mother-f@#Kers'* and *'mother-f@#King'* found in Slavic, Balkan, Arabic, Latin and Chinese languages!

But when it comes to swearing the Dutch stand alone. Of course, they have a handful of dirty words relating to religion (*godverdomme, hel, Jezus Christus*) and sexuality (*lul, klootzak, eikel, kut*)... but the mother of all Dutch swear words is the Big C.

Yes, Dutch people like to swear with diseases. Better yet, they often swear with dreaded diseases from the past. In fact, they go so far as to make angry bold statements wishing these diseases upon you or cursing you with a particular deadly ailment. The more serious your offense, the more serious the disease in question. If you are going to spend any time in the Netherlands, you had better brush up on your knowledge of rare diseases from years gone by.

Typhoid, tuberculosis, cholera, smallpox, the plague and the Big C (cancer, that is) can all rear their ugly heads when tempers fly.

NO BLOODY
SWEARING

This "swearing-by-disease" is a unique Dutch trait. No other language has similar curses. It's odd and it's strange and quite frankly, pretty darn harsh. "*I hope you get smallpox and die*" – certainly doesn't beat around the bush and nothing packs a punch quite like *Sterf aan kanker*! ('Die of cancer'!). Furthermore, diseases can often be combined to double (or triple) their effect, for instance: '*godverdomse tyfus pleuris kankerzooi*' (translation: 'goddamned typhus pleurisy cancer-mess'). Go ahead, have some fun, and make up your own combinations - but be forewarned, they aren't for the faint of heart!

A shortlist of Dutch nasty words

krijg de kanker	get cancer
krijg de pest	catch the plague
krijg de klere	get cholera
kankeren	"to cancer" is a verb meaning "to complain excessively"
pestkop	"plague head", is someone who engages in bullying
takke	from the French *attaque* is a slang word for stroke. *Krijg de takke* , "have a stroke", is used as an insult.
teringlijer	slang word for "tuberculosis sufferer"

GUESS WHO INVENTED ENGLISH?

The Dutch of course! Hundreds of English words come directly from the Dutch language. Now go eat a *cookie* on your *yacht* like *a boss*!

JAMES Cagney

YANKEE DOODLE DANDY

Based on the story of
GEORGE M. COHAN
with the Greatest of all his Great Music

JOAN LESLIE
WALTER HUSTON
RICHARD WHORF

JEANNE CAGNEY • FRANCES LANGFORD
GEORGE TOBIAS • IRENE MANNING

Directed by
MICHAEL CURTIZ

Lyrics and Music by
GEORGE M. COHAN

Presented by WARNER BROS.

Yankee

This term originates from 17th century New York (New Amsterdam) where it was used by Dutch settlers as a derogatory name for the English colonists in neighboring Connecticut. The word "Yankee" may come from the Dutch name *Janke* (a diminutive of the name Jan) or from the name *Jan Kes* (a familiar form of Jan Cornelius). Others believe it comes instead from the name *Jan Kaas* ("John Cheese") which was a generic nickname, at the time, for the Dutch. It seems the term was first used insultingly towards the Dutch, who later turned it around on the English themselves!

Coleslaw

The English word "coleslaw" is a bastardization of the Dutch word *koolsla*. The Dutch word literally translates to "cabbage salad". And there you were thinking all along that this word was utterly weird! Look who's hungry for some fried chicken and coleslaw now!

Boss

It turns out the Dutch also invented the expression "*like a boss*"! Well, indirectly that is. The Dutch word *baas* was first used in the 1620's as the standard title for a ship's captain. The Americans may have taken the word on as their own to avoid the use of the word "master" which implied slave subordinates rather than free labourers.

Brandy

I love a good Cognac on a cold Dutch night. Little did I know that "brandy" (brandywine) got its name from the Dutch word *brandewijn*, meaning "burned wine" (referring to the distilling process). Bottoms up!

Booze

Booze - the word oozes fun, but where o' where does it come from? This slang word for alcohol comes from the old Dutch verb *busen* which meant to "drink heavily".

FUN FACT :
The origin of the word "booze" is often mistakenly credited to E.C. Booz. Mr Booz was an American alcohol distiller in the 19th century, however, his appropriate surname was simply a happy coincidence as the Dutch word predates him!

Santa Claus

It's no fairytale that the modern day figure of Santa Claus is derived from the Dutch *Sinterklaas*. Sinterklaas was named after St. Nicolaus, the Bishop of Mira, who lived in Turkey in the 3rd century. According to the legend, he saved the town from starvation, revived a couple of dead children, and offered gifts of dowries to poor girls so they didn't have to become prostitutes: a pretty saintly dude.

It is often claimed that during the American War of Independence, the inhabitants of New York City (which was a former Dutch colonial town) reinvented the Sinterklaas tradition. In 1773 the *New York Gazetteer* first made reference to a celebration of 'St. A Claus' by the descendants of the ancient Dutch families. You say Sinterklaas, I say Santa Claus... let's call the whole thing off! ☺

Cookie

The word "cookie" is directly borrowed from the Dutch word *koekje* (biscuit/cookie), which is pronounced *kook-ye*.

FUN FACT :
The English spelling of Dutch words typically omitted combinations of vowels which do not exist in English (like "oe") and replaced them with existing vowel combinations respectively (like "oo"). Hence, the **oe** in *koekje* became **oo** in *cookie.*

Cruise

The origin of this word is the Dutch verb *kruisen*, which means "to cross" or to "sail to and fro". With the Dutch being one of the leading seafaring nations it's no wonder so many English words relating to the sea or sailing (such as "sloop", "buoy", "deck", "pump", "bow", "skipper" and "yacht") have their origins in the Lowlands.

Skate

With the Dutch's dominance in Olympic skating, it's no wonder they invented the word! It is said that the word (derived from the Dutch word *schaats*) was brought to England in the 1660s by the exiled followers of King Charles the Second who had taken refuge in the Netherlands.

Quack

The word "quack" is defined as *"a person who pretends to have skill, knowledge, or qualifications he or she does not possess"* or a *"medical charlatan"*. The word is derived from the now obsolete Dutch word *quacksalver* (spelled *kwakzalver* in contemporary Dutch). *Kwakzalver* literally means "hawker of salve" (salve being a medical ointment).

Landscape

The English word "landscape" comes directly from the Dutch word *landschap* (which is a combination of Dutch words *land* and *ship*). The word's association with scenery came about in the late 16th century when it was first used by Dutch painters to describe paintings of rural/inland imagery.

Spooky

This Dutch word, and its variations, made its way into the English language as early as 1801. *Spook*, in Dutch, is defined as a "spectre, apparition or ghost". In English, it is used as a verb, as in "*to frighten a person or animal*" (e.g "After the horror film, he was spooked!") or an adjective (*spooky*) meaning "*sinister or ghostly in a way that causes fear and unease*".

DOUBLE DUTCH

You'll need some "Dutch courage" to suggest "going Dutch" to my friend. He can be a real "Dutch uncle" about these things. Oh, and don't ask him about his "Dutch wife" or he might start talking "Double Dutch"!

The Dutch should be proud. Very proud. For such a tiny little country, they've managed to successfully infiltrate and influence the English language.
Have you ever noticed how often the Dutch are referenced in English expressions? No? Well, it's time to listen up!

Unfortunately, the majority of English expressions using the word "Dutch" aren't really on the positive side. Most of them in fact, pack quite the punch and seem to foster more than a little animosity towards the Dutch.

Why so? Well, the Dutch had quite a prolific history of seafaring, trade and war. The Anglo-Dutch wars of the 17th and 18th centuries resulted in the Brits not feeling too much love towards the Dutchies and vice versa. These phrases reflected the English opinion of the time when the Dutch were considered to be a slightly boozy, slightly cheap folk that were not to be trusted. Of course, there are also a lot of words and phrases derived from the Dutch settlers in America, these, luckily, are slightly more kind!

Let's look at a few of our favourites:

Double Dutch

It is said that the English found the Dutch language so incredibly difficult to understand, that the saying "Double Dutch" came to stand for anything that was utterly incomprehensible (i.e. even twice as hard as Dutch)!

Over the years, oddly enough, the term was adopted in various other realms and now can refer to:

1. an incomprehensible language
2. a made-up language similar to Pig Latin
3. a game or jump rope that involves two ropes moving in opposite directions, played by one or two jumpers*
4. using both a condom and the birth control pill - just to be on the *uber* safe side 🙂 *(colloquial)*

it is widely debated whether the game came to America with the first Dutch settlers or whether it was a homegrown sport.

Dutch doors

This term is used to describe a door that is divided horizontally in two, so that it can either open at the top or bottom (although usually just the top). The Dutch invented this type of door to let sunshine/air in without letting the kids out or animals in. The term was since adopted in some English-speaking circles to mean "bi-sexual", as in "he/she swings both ways".

Dutch uncle

To call someone a "Dutch uncle" is far from a compliment. In fact, if this name is flung your way it may mean you dispense *"frank, harsh, critical or rude comments"* in order to *"educate, encourage, or admonish someone"*. Rather the opposite of what someone would look for in an uncle!

Dutch wife

A "Dutch wife" is a long pillow that can be held or wrapped around one's body while sleeping. The origin of this term is thought to be from Dutch sailors who would spend long periods away from their wives, with only their pillows to cuddle. In more recent days, the term has also been applied to inflatable sex dolls, particularly those made in Asia. Warning: Your Dutch wife won't be amused if you bring home a "Dutch wife".

Dutch treat

This little term is actually the exact opposite of what it sounds. A "Dutch treat" is when you are asked out for dinner and expect to be treated by the other, only to be asked to pay for yourself! Some date!

Going Dutch

This common expression, meaning to pay for one's own food or to split the bill at a restaurant, is known to North Americans from coast to coast. The expression is often interpreted to mean the Dutch are either a) really cheap or b) value equality (in reference to splitting the bill in equal parts).

**Are the Dutch cheap? We polled our community
and here's what they said:**

"I don't look at it as being cheap. I just look at it in the sense that I am preventing 'financial waste'. "

"It's about spending on things that are important to you. My Dutch boyfriend will keep looking for the cheapest parking lot in town, yet gladly spend €2000 on a flight ticket in business class."

"My Dutch parents survived WW II and taught their children: if you cannot afford it – don't buy it. Lending money – costs money... and you can only spend your money once! "

Dutch courage

The term "Dutch courage" has come to represent booze induced bravery and is now used interchangeably with "liquid courage". There are two popular versions as to how this term came about. The first states that Dutch gin was used by English soldiers before they went into battle. The second version is a little less positive and states that Dutch soldiers had to rely on alcohol to overcome their lack of bravery.

Dutch bargain

A Dutch bargain is a deal/bargain made when you are drunk, too drunk to know better. The first recorded use of the term in English was in 1654. This phrase is again from the time of the English/Dutch rivalry, when many an Englishman may have made poor deals while under the influence.

And the list (of unfavourable terms) goes on...

Dutch oven	Originally a cast iron pot, this term has taken up another meaning recently. A Dutch oven now often refers to when one farts and traps their partner under the blankets to enjoy the smell. Look it up. We kid you not!
Dutch defence	a legal tactic whereby you rat someone out in order to get off free (first recorded in 1749)
Dutch gold	a false gold made of copper and zinc (brass), worthless in itself
Dutch wallet	nickname for someone who is cheap
Dutch blessing	a scolding/a lecture
Dutch widow	a prostitute (17th century British slang)

Ze vonderful vorld of Dunglish

What do you get when you mix a little Dutch with a lot of English: why, Dunglish, of course! Welcome to this wonderful world of wacky words. Don't say we didn't warn you!

De zuigers zijn buiten werking.

De directie

The suckers are out working.

The direction

DUNGLISH!

We need to preface this chapter with the following statement: The Dutch, in the vast majority of cases, speak English very well. In fact, they speak it waaay better than their European counterparts. Put an average Dutch, French, Spanish, Greek and German person in a room and you are sure to find that the Dutch will be chatting away speaking the best English by far!

Why is this? How did the Dutch linguistically soar ahead of their peers? The answer is a combination of education and exposure. English is a compulsory subject in all Dutch secondary institutions, with many Dutch children already learning English in elementary school. Additionally, the Dutch have a secret weapon exposing them to a steady stream of English from a very young age: the television! Unlike their French or German neighbours, the Dutch broadcast English/American shows in English with Dutch subtitles - no awkward time-delayed voice-overs for these folks!

Herein lies the problem - the Dutch speak English a little too well. Too well, you ask? How could that possibly be?! Let me explain: the Dutch speak and understand English so well, that at times they have been known to get a little ahead of themselves. They get a little over confident in their abilities and start, well, making up all kinds of crazy shit! Words that don't exist, suddenly do; grammar goes out the window; and word order is flipped upside down! To make matters worse, all of this is done in a supremely confident tone, often even confusing a native-English speaker on its accuracy. *If it looks like English and smells like English, it must be...* But beware my friends: this is not English at all. This is... Dunglish!

Dunglish is exactly what it sounds like. It's mostly English, with a distinctly sneaky Dutch influence. After living nearly a decade in this country I myself can sometimes even fall prey to Dunglish's persuasive ways.

You seem to be having a perfectly normal English conversation until BOOM, something goes terribly awry. You hear English words, yet their meaning is a blur. The results are confusing, disorienting, and often hilarious.

Shoes out for that you enters this space

Ruimte   coordinator

LET OP
deur op
slot glas
wordt mat

ATTENTION
lock door
transparency
will cease
to be

"COAL ENGLISH?!"

The Dutch have long since acknowledged this phenomena, even coining their own term *steenkolenengels*. This "Coal English" is said to have originated in the early twentieth century when Dutch harbour workers devised their own form of "English" in an attempt to communicate with the docking British coal ships.

Dunglish can take the form of wonky words, literal translations and mistaken "false friends". "False friends" occur when a word is mistranslated, for understandable reasons (i.e. the original words appearing very similar). Over the course of history, Dunglish (and its "false friends") has been said to have often reared its head even in the most important of situations.

HISTORIC DUNGLISH :

1 Former Dutch Prime Minister Joop den Uyl once famously said in an English speech that *"the Dutch are a nation of undertakers"*. Mistakenly using a literal translation for the Dutch word "entrepreneurs" (*ondernemers*), and referring instead to *begrafenisondernemer* (*undertakers*)! Oops!!

2 Former Dutch Prime Minister Pieter Sjoerds Gerbrandy is said to have had greeted Winston Churchill in London by saying *"Good day!"* (translating the Dutch "goedendag" to English). Churchill responded: "This is the shortest meeting I have ever had!". *Good day* is often used in English on departure, such as "goodbye", rather than arrival!

3 A Dutch minister speaking at an energy conference supposedly once said: *"We always use gas from our bottom"* (loosely translating *"gas uit de bodem"*, meaning from the ground). The attendees must have been really impressed that the Dutch had finally succeeded in harvesting and utilizing human-made gas!

It's hard to tell fact from fiction, as many a folk will tell you of the hilarious historic exchange between the Dutch foreign minister Joseph Luns and President Kennedy.

When Kennedy supposedly asked Luns if he had any hobbies, Luns replied "*I fok horses*" (mistakenly using the Dutch verb *fokken* which means 'breeding'). The story goes that Kennedy was taken aback by this proclamation and said "Pardon?", with Luns replying "*Yes, paarden!*" (Yes, horses!!)

Did this conversation actually happen? I suppose we may never really know, but what's for certain, is that the mixing of Dutch and English can result in a heck of a lot of laughs!

Let's have a look at some more beautiful real life Dunglish examples:

155

Out of Order

Sorry for the incontinence

Van wie is de NR 39

Vuilniszak !!!!

Graag opruimen !!!

NR 39 v/d koop !   NR 39 !

From who are
the garbage !!!
Like cleaning !!!

No passage!

Trap is painted

Geen doorgang !

Trap is geschilderd.

Paarden Uitdeelplaats

Pfeerde Ausgabe platz

Horse Expend place

NIET ROKEN BIJ HET RAAM A.U.B.
MAAR BIJ DE ROOKZUIL.

UW ROOK TREKT DE KAMER IN. WIJ
HEBBEN HIER LAST VAN !!!

ROKEN VOOR DE INGANG VAN EEN
GEBOUW IS VERBODEN !!!

DO NOT SMOKE BESIDE THE
WINDOWS OF THIS ROOMS

ONLY FOR A SMOKE COLUMN.
YOUR SMOKE COMES THROUGH THE ROOM
AT THE SPLIT.
WE HAVE THERE PROBLEMS WITH !!!

SMOKING FOR THE ENTRANCE OF A
BUILDING IS PROHIBITED !!!

Bij storing van de Koffieautomaat direct bellen
AUB NIET ZELF HET PROBLEEM OPLOSSEN

Automaatnummer 101771
Lokatie waar koffiemachine staat 2B01

Upon the failure of coffee machine directly call.
PLEASE DO NOT OWN THE PROBLEM SOLVING

Automaatnummer 101771
Location where coffee is 2B01

Suikerbrood

Sacker bread
€ 0.75

NIET OPENEN , STAAT ALARM OP !! ALLEEN BIJ BRAND

ALARMDOOR, NOT OPENEN PLEASE !! ALONE BY FIRE

Plastic bottles, cardboard, paper, look.

Like the plastic bottles flat stairs please!!!

Plastic flessen, karton, papier blik.

Graag de plastic flessen plat trappen aub!!!

Van Gaalisms

Dutch football manager Louis Van Gaal is the #1 International Ambassador of Dunglish, spreading his love of befuddled English worldwide. Can't understand him? It's not his fault, it's yours! His war on English is real and he's not taking any prisoners.

Best of Van Gaal

It's a gladiolus game.
Or you are dead or you receive
the gladiolus flower. It's like
that. In cup matches,
it's always like that

When you analyzed the games,
then we have twitched our ass on the
bench. [...] I said to my players I was
squeezing my ass, but that was the wrong
expression [...] You can go back, it was
always twitching your ass.
And I don't like that.

Congratulations on signing the best coach in the world. (To an Ajax director, after signing his first contract as coach.)

Am I the one who's so smart, or are you so stupid? (After a journalist had asked him a question.)

I've never worn leggings like Robben does. I'm never cold because I'm warm blooded. My wife says so too. We always sleep spooning.

And then you are always running behind the facts.

Now we have to play against Chelsea. In the Netherlands they say "that is another cook"

Running is for animals. You need a brain and a ball for football.

I've signed a contract with the Dutch national team until 2006, so I can win the World Cup not once but twice. (Van Gaal in 2000. He failed to even qualify for the 2002 World Cup and then quit as NL coach.)

A literal people

literal, lɪt(ə)r(ə)l/
adjective

1. Taking words in their usual or most basic sense without metaphor or exaggeration.

2. The Dutch

WHAT AN ANGLOPHONE SAYS	WHAT HE/SHE MEANS
How are you?	Hello!
Correct me if I'm wrong, but...	I'm right
That's not bad	That's quite good to very good
Perhaps you would like to think about...	I would really suggest you think about this
I was a bit disappointed that	I am quite upset with you
Please think about that some more	Bad idea, please reconsider

WHAT A DUTCH PERSON UNDERSTANDS

He wants a truthful answer about my state of being

She is unsure of what she is saying

That's mediocre at best

A suggestion but I can do as I like

Not really important

They like the idea!

WHAT AN ANGLOPHONE SAYS	WHAT HE/SHE MEANS
That's interesting	I might be mildly interested
You must come for dinner sometime	Just being polite (not an actual invite)
That is an original point of view	You're just silly
I hear you	I agree with you
In my humble opinion (IMHO)	I'm not really humble and you're wrong
See you later	Good bye
Good for you	I'm happy for you

WHAT A DUTCH PERSON UNDERSTANDS

They're impressed

I will receive an invitation tomorrow

They like my ideas!

Not sure if she agrees or not...

He's unsure of his position

I will see her again today

He's making fun of me

WHAT AN ANGLOPHONE SAYS	WHAT HE/SHE MEANS
I'll think about it	I won't change my position
With all due respect	Listen to me, you idiot. You probably won't understand, but here it goes
Let's do lunch	Bye Bye

WHAT A DUTCH PERSON UNDERSTANDS

There is a chance she will see my point

He is wavering

Let's pull out our calendars and schedule a date right now

From our community

My mum and I were in the Netherlands (my mum was born in Amsterdam, I was born in Australia), from June - September. My mum went and visited one of her uncles one day, about an hour out of Amsterdam. She mentioned to him (an 80 year old man), that it would be lovely for him to come and stay with us (as in, for a few days/week), if he ever decided to travel to Australia. Six weeks on, guess who is now PERMANENTLY LIVING with us, having interpreted "come and stay with us" to "buy a one-way ticket to Brisbane and come and live with your niece and her daughter permanently". Really, is this REALLY my life??

When i was 14 years old i went on holiday to the States. Once at the mall a lady told me "your welcome " so i said "aww thank you that is very sweet to say" ... got a weird look in return. And at the counter "Hi, how are you?" So I told the lady i was there on holiday with my grandmother and blahblahblah..." Yep got another strange look.

My mum was on a walk to Santiago where she saw a young man with huge backpacks. She said to him: You have great sacks! He answered: I wish.

My first time in aussie.... the girl in the supermarket said to me.."no worries" (after i said thank you to her when i got my change)... i said to her..."no no i don't have worries".

Seems to me the English are talking double dutch...

When we lived in Utrecht we met our neighbour outside, cleaning his car. In a jokey sort of way my husband said "you can do mine when you've finished that" and our lovely neighbour replied, very apologetically, "I'm sorry, I don't think I'll have time".

A colleague of mine wanted to ask a customer how he and his family are. He said: `Enneeh, how are you doing with your wife?`

WISDOM ON A TILE?

The Dutch have been doling out words of wisdom on pretty blue tiles (*tegelspreuken*) since the 16th century. That's a pretty long time, so listen up my friends, as it turns out "No one receives a program for the concert of life" (Popular *tegelspreuken*: *"van het concert des levens krijgt niemand een program"*)

East, west, home is best!

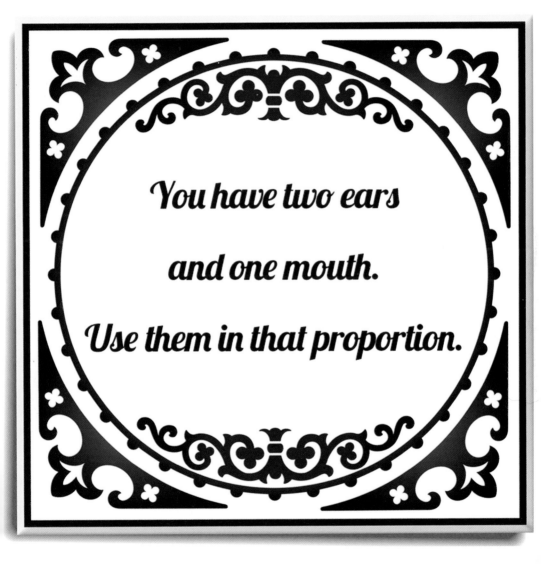

You have two ears

and one mouth.

Use them in that proportion.

When one door closes another opens.

Or you can open the closed door. That's how doors work.

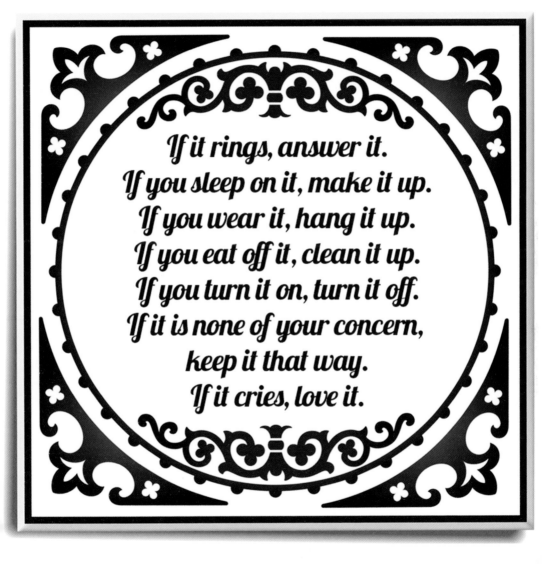

If it rings, answer it.
If you sleep on it, make it up.
If you wear it, hang it up.
If you eat off it, clean it up.
If you turn it on, turn it off.
If it is none of your concern,
keep it that way.
If it cries, love it.

Gezelligheid kent geen tijd.

The clock doesn't tick the same anywhere like it does at home.

On the journey to happiness there is no elevator only stairs.

Life is like picking your nose.
You gotta get out what you can.

Who doesn't value the small things, doesn't deserve the big ones.

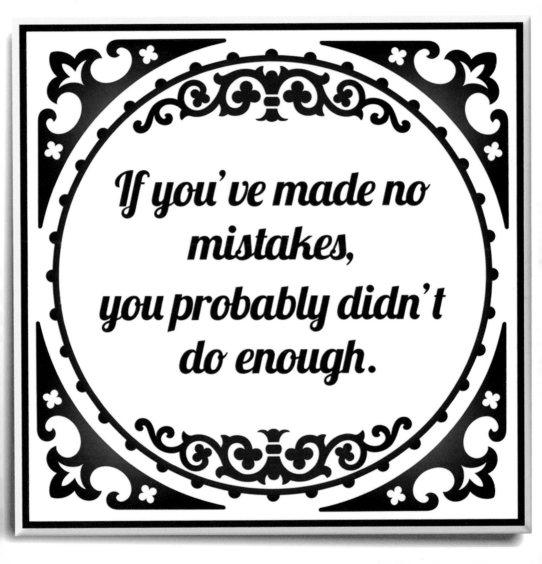

If you've made no mistakes, you probably didn't do enough.

EHBO

afz.

ZOZ

KEEPING IT SHORT

The Dutch are tall. In fact, they are the tallest people on the planet. Because of this, they can afford to keep a lot of their words short. Take a peek at all this tiny talk.

ABBREV	WHAT IT MEANS	TRANSLATION
afz.	afzender	sender
alg.	algemeen	general
a.s.	aanstaande	coming (as in coming Friday)
aso	asociaal	anti-social behaviour or person
aub	alstublieft	please
begr.	begraven	buried
beh	behalve	except for
BTW	Belasting Toegevoegde Waarde	VAT
ca	circa	around
dag	dagelijks	daily
dd	de dato (Latin)	dated from
dhr	de heer	Sir
dir.	directeur	CEO
dmv	door middel van	by means of
dwz	dat wil zeggen	i.e.

ABBREV	WHAT IT MEANS	TRANSLATION
EHBO	Eerste Hulp Bij Ongelukken	First Aid
enz	enzovoorts	et cetera
exc	exclusief	exclusive of
geb.	geboren	date of birth
gesch.	gescheiden	divorced
idd	inderdaad	indeed
igvn	in geval van nood	in case of emergency
iha	in het algemeen	generally
iig	in ieder geval	in any case
ipv	in plaats van	instead of
itt	in tegenstelling tot	in contrast with
ivm	in verband met	in connection with
j.l.	jongstleden	last (e.g. last Thursday)
k.k.	kosten koper	costs charged to the buyer (of a house)
KvK	Kamer van Koophandel	Chamber of Commerce

ABBREV	WHAT IT MEANS	TRANSLATION
L.S.	lectori salutem (Latin)	To whom it may concern (on letter)
m.b.t.	met betrekking tot	concerning
miv	met ingang van	from/since (date/time)
muv	met uitzondering van	with the exception of
M/V	man/vrouw	man/woman
mv	meervoud	plural
m.vr.gr.	met vriendelijke groeten	with kind regards (letter)
Mw	mevrouw	Madam, Mrs
nav	naar aanleiding van	as a result of
notk	nader overeen te komen	to be agreed
nl	namelijk	namely
o.a.	onder andere	amongst other things
o.l.v.	onder leiding van	supervised by
o.m.	onder meer	including
ong.	ongeveer	approximately

ABBREV	WHAT IT MEANS	TRANSLATION
oorspr.	oorspronkelijk	originally
overl.	overleden	deceased
tgv	ten gevolge van	as a result of
t/m	tot en met	up to and including
tnv	ten name van	in the name of
tov	ten opzichte van	compared to
twv	ter waarde van	valued at
v.a.	vanaf	from (mostly used for pricing)
vnl	voornamelijk	mainly
Wvttk	Wat verder ter tafel komt	additional items added to an agenda during business meetings
Zgan	zo goed als nieuw	as good as new
zgn.	zogenaamd	as a matter of speaking
z.s.m	zo spoedig mogelijk	ASAP
zoz	zie ommezijde	see other side

ABOUT US

Colleen Geske is the author of the hugely popular blog 'Stuff Dutch People Like'. She is originally from Winnipeg, Canada and has lived in Europe since 2004. When not busy writing, Colleen spends her days as a communications and social media consultant. Colleen holds a Bachelor of Commerce (Honours) degree in International Business and Marketing from the University of Manitoba. She currently lives in Amsterdam with her family.

Stuff Dutch People Like (The Original)

If you like this book, make sure to also check out our bestselling guide to all things orange: **Stuff Dutch People Like**.

Blunt, provocative and wickedly funny, *Stuff Dutch People Like* is a satirical look at Dutch culture as seen through the eyes of an outsider. From *Appelmoes* to *Zwarte Piet* and everything in between, *Stuff Dutch People Like* covers it all – and then some!

Stuff Dutch People Like is a celebration of the Lowlands and its peculiar inhabitants. With thousands of books sold and over 300,000 Facebook fans, *Stuff Dutch People Like* has struck a nerve!

Photo Credits

Page	Creator	Source	License Type
p12	Photocapy	https://www.flickr.com/photos/photocapy/416593901/	CC BY-SA 2.0
p15	Online Dialogue	https://www.flickr.com/photos/onlinedialogue/6838709178/	CC BY-SA 2.0
p108	Patrik Theander	https://www.flickr.com/photos/fabolous/8627113727/	CC BY-SA 2.0
p111	Steffen Köhler	https://www.flickr.com/photos/baertierchen/9309228413/	CC BY-SA 2.0
p116	Cliff	https://www.flickr.com/photos/nostri-imago/2869508678/	CC BY 2.0
p119	Setven Depolo	https://www.flickr.com/photos/stevendepolo/6738316555/	CC BY 2.0
p120	Shaylor	https://www.flickr.com/photos/shaylor/7426883/in/photostream/	CC BY-ND 2.0
p123	Andreas Kohn	https://www.flickr.com/photos/15341182@N00/6363067651/	CC BY 2.0
p124	Martijn van Exel	https://www.flickr.com/photos/rhodes/6873340785/	CC BY-SA 2.0
p127	Michiel Jelijs	https://www.flickr.com/photos/thewolf/6865132503/	CC BY 2.0
p128	Frans Berkelaar	https://www.flickr.com/photos/28169156@N03/19956928653/	CC BY-SA 2.0
p134	Angel Schatz	https://www.flickr.com/photos/glamourschatz/1186032219/	CC BY 2.0
p137	Paul Flint & Company	https://www.flickr.com/photos/pflintandco/7461289802/	CC BY-SA 2.0
p141	Sam Howzit	https://www.flickr.com/photos/aloha75/8398636830/	CC BY 2.0
p142	singingbeagle	https://www.flickr.com/photos/singingbeagle/3701966102/	CC BY-SA 2.0